—Weird and Wacky Science—

MUMMIES

Ron Knapp

ENSLOW PUBLISHERS, INC.

44 Fadem Road	P.O. Box 38
Box 699	Aldershot
Springfield, N.J. 07081	Hants GU12 6BP
U.S.A.	U.K.

Library of Congress Cataloging-in-Publication Data

Knapp, Ron.
    Mummies / by Ron Knapp.
       p. cm. — (Weird and wacky science)
    Includes bibliographical references (p.) and index.
    Summary: Discusses the process of mummification as well as the individual histories of
four real mummies—The Iceman, King Tut, Tollund Man, and The Lady—and of plaster
mummies from Pompeii and how they have advanced historical and scientific knowledge.
    ISBN 0-89490-618-6
    1. Mummies—Juvenile literature. [1. Mummies.] I. Title.
    II. Series.
    GN293K63 1996
    393'.3—dc20   94-42691
                                            CIP
                                            AC

Printed in the United States of America

10 9 8 7 6 5 4 3 2 1

Illustration Credits: © Andrew Blair/Tradd Street Stock, p. 12; Enslow
Publishers, Inc., p. 15; Forschunginstitut für Alpine Vorzeit/Gehwolf, pp. 8, 10;
Forschunginstitut für Alpine Vorzeit/Maurer, p. 4; Griffith Institute, Ashmolean
Museum, Oxford, pp. 18, 23; © Charles O'Rear/Westlight, pp. 36, 41; Scala/Art
Resource, Egyptian Museum, Cairo, pp. 16, 21; Scala/Art Resource, p. 24;
Silkeborg Museum, Denmark, pp. 33, 35; © John Verde/Photo Researchers, Inc.,
p. 28; VU/© Albert J. Copely, p. 27; VU/© Will Troyer, p. 30.

Cover Photo: © Mary Morina/Unicorn Stock Photos.

Contents

The Iceman stares back at us from nearly five thousand years ago.

1

THE ICEMAN

It was cold, and the shepherd was tired.[1] He and his sheep were passing through the Alps, a mountain range in Europe. When he looked down into the valley, he could see the autumn leaves turning bright colors. There were no trees where he was; he and the sheep were too high.

The shepherd wished they were in the valley now. The winds wouldn't be so cold, and he would be closer to home. The valley was several hours away, though, and he was too tired to go on. If he could only rest for a while, he would have the strength to go on.

The shepherd had been in the mountains before, and he knew how to dress. His coat was made of deerskin. A fur hat was strapped under his chin. His leggings were made of animal skin.

The grass stuffed inside his calfskin shoes helped keep his feet warm. The shepherd had woven long reeds together to make a cape that he wore on top of his other clothing, but he was still very cold. He wanted to get out of the icy wind. Up ahead he saw a trench. It was about six feet deep and twenty feet long, perfect for protection from the cold.

He climbed with the sheep down into the trench, and he no longer felt the wind. Then he began unloading all the equipment he was carrying. First he set down the six-foot bow he had carved out of a branch. When he got home, he would string it with the animal tendons he carried in his pouch. He took off his deerskin quiver filled with the fourteen arrows he was working on. Next to him on the ground he put his most important possession, an ax made from a metal blade and a wooden handle. Still tucked into his clothes were the clumps of moss he used as we would use toilet paper.

Then the shepherd pulled his supper out of the pouch he wore on his belt. He probably used his flint knife to rip off a chunk of meat from an ibex he had killed earlier in his journey. For dessert he had a few berries.

Now that his stomach was full and he was out of the wind, he lay down on a long rock in the middle of the trench. When he woke up, he and his sheep would finish their journey down the mountain.

But the shepherd never woke up. His sheep wandered away, and he was alone. Soon a blizzard blew in and he was covered with snow. By then he was dead. Within a few hours, his body was frozen. The shepherd was now the Iceman. But the snow kept coming, and after a few years he was buried under a glacier. That's where he stayed for five thousand years.

It was as if the shepherd's body had been put into a freezer. He just sat there, frozen stiff, waiting to be thawed out. Over the centuries the weather stayed cold and he stayed frozen. Huge, heavy glaciers slid over the mountain, but he was protected in the trench. His body was never crushed or ripped apart by the moving ice.

The Iceman Is Found

The Iceman might have remained frozen forever, but in March 1991 there was a violent storm over the Sahara Desert. Dust blew north from Africa to Europe. Some of it settled on his mountain. The dark dust absorbed much more heat from the sun than the white snow ever had. Soon the top layers of ice were melting. Finally, for the first time in fifty centuries, the sun was shining again on the Iceman.

He was found on September 19, 1991, by a pair of German mountain climbers. At first they thought they were looking at the head and shoulders of a doll sticking out of the ice. But when they got closer, they could see that the Iceman was human. In fact, his frozen eyeballs were staring back at them.

At first nobody was really concerned about the body found in the ice. It wasn't unusual for skiers and climbers to become lost in the Alps. Frozen bodies were often found whenever the weather warmed and a few inches of the snow melted. The Iceman didn't appear to be anything special. He was dressed in a deerskin coat and had a fur cap over his head. On his belt was a pouch that looked a lot like a modern fanny bag.

Soon after the discovery several hikers climbed up the

Rescuers jabbed the ice around the body with ski poles. They didn't realize the Iceman was nearly 5,000 years old. While trying to free the body from the ice, some parts were damaged.

mountain to have a look at the Iceman. They chopped at the ice with ski poles and axes in an attempt to free the rest of the body. While they worked, they broke the frame of his backpack and snapped his bow. Some of them ripped off pieces of his coat for souvenirs. An impatient policeman brought up a jackhammer to finish the job. It blasted away a chunk of the Iceman's hip. It took four days to get him out of the ice. During that time the exposed parts of his body thawed out each day in the warm sun, then froze again at night.

Scientists Go to Work

Rainer Henn, a forensic expert, was probably the first to suspect that the Iceman wasn't just another frozen skier. "When I saw this knife," he said, "I had the idea that this man was very old." The knife had a wooden handle and a blade made out of a piece of flint just over an inch long. Flint was the rock used by many ancient peoples for arrowheads. "From that moment I ordered all the people to be most careful while getting the body out of the ice."[2]

Once the body was free, it was packed in a bag and flown to a nearby Austrian village. There the left arm was broken when it was stuffed into a coffin for a car ride to Innsbruck. For thousands of years the Iceman's body had been undamaged, but in four days, the rescuers had almost wrecked it.

Konrad Spindler, an archaeologist in Innsbruck, was shocked when he saw the Iceman. "I needed only one second," he said, "to see that the body was four thousand years old."[3] It was the ax that caught his attention. The four-inch blade appeared to be bronze. Leather thongs soaked in tree sap held it to the handle. Spindler knew bronze tools were used around 2000 B.C.

To prevent decay, the Iceman's body is kept in a moisture-free freezer. It is similar to the hollow in the Alpine glacier that preserved his body for so many centuries.

When the ax was examined more closely, the blade was found to be made of copper. Hot, melted liquid had been poured into a mold, then cooled and hammered into shape. Prehistoric men in Europe had used copper long before they had used bronze. The experts finally decided that the Iceman had lived around 3000 B.C. His was the oldest preserved body ever found.

Clues From Droppings and Teeth

In 1992, scientists returned to the Iceman's trench. They discovered a piece of his longbow and traces of animal droppings, most likely from sheep. That's what made them decide he had probably been a shepherd.

Other scientists have continued to examine the body itself. Using X rays, they found that he was probably in his late twenties or early thirties when he lay down in the trench. He stood five feet, two inches tall, about average for his time. Since his teeth were very worn, they determined that his main food was a tough, gritty bread. The groove in his left ear showed that at some time he must have worn an earring. He also had four sets of tattoos: a cross on his left knee, fourteen small stripes down his lower back, and four three-inch stripes on the top of his left foot. "His clothing would have covered the tattoos," said Spindler. "They were not meant to be seen publicly."[4] So what was the purpose of the tattoos? Nobody knows.

Today the body of the Iceman rests in a freezer in Innsbruck, Austria. It is occasionally still brought out for a few moments so scientists can further examine it. The mysteries of a man who died five thousand years ago are still being unraveled.

This mummy was found in the Alto Plano desert of Bolivia. At 12,500 feet above sea level, the dryness of the desert preserved the body.

♦ 2 ♦
BODIES THAT DON'T DECAY

When people and animals die, their bodies begin to decay. Bacteria breaks down the flesh and organs. After a few months, there is nothing left but bones.

Modern people have developed methods to embalm, or preserve, bodies. Blood is removed and replaced by a fluid containing formaldehyde, a chemical that prevents decay. There is nothing new about preserving bodies; people have been doing it for thousands of years. Bodies from the past that haven't decayed are called mummies.

Sometimes mummies are formed naturally. If conditions are right, very dry air, severe cold, or bogs can preserve bodies. Some societies have gone to a lot of trouble to create mummies on purpose. Usually for religious reasons, they want bodies to remain intact. Modern scientists have made mummies of their own combining bones and plaster.

Mummies give us unique clues to the lives and cultures of the people who came before us. By examining their teeth, scientists can determine the texture of the food they ate. Sometimes it's possible to examine their final meal by looking into what's left of their stomachs. The condition of the skin and bones reveals whether or not the person had to do tough, physical labor.

Clothing and other artifacts found with the mummies offer information as well. The moss "toilet paper" found with the Iceman has convinced many experts that he had just come from what is now the Italian side of the Alps.[1] That is the only place that particular moss grows. We can discover how the ancient people hunted by examining their weapons.

From carefully prepared mummies, we learn a lot about what their societies considered important. None of them would have gone to the trouble of preserving bodies if they had not believed in an afterlife. These bodies were being prepared for a new life in a place modern people call heaven.

Some of the religious beliefs we discover seem strange, even troubling, to us. What kind of a god would demand human sacrifices? How could anybody believe that statues and slaughtered animals were going to come to life to serve the mummies they surrounded?

We would know much more about the ancient world if the first discoverers of the mummies had been more careful. Many Egyptian mummies were stomped to dust or ground up to be used as medicine. Robbers stole almost all of the treasures left in tombs. Even modern discoveries are sometimes damaged before scientists arrive on the scene.

The mummies and the other evidence that is left can't answer all our questions. We're not even sure how all of them died. The search for more evidence and more answers goes on. While you are reading this book, archaeologists around the world continue to dig for more mummies and other clues to the past. Scientists in laboratories continue to examine the ancient bodies already found.

At the same time, thousands of people view the discoveries in museums around the world. They are fascinated by the artifacts once used by ancient peoples. The mummies themselves are always the most popular exhibits. History comes alive when you look into the face of somebody who's been dead for hundreds or thousands of years.

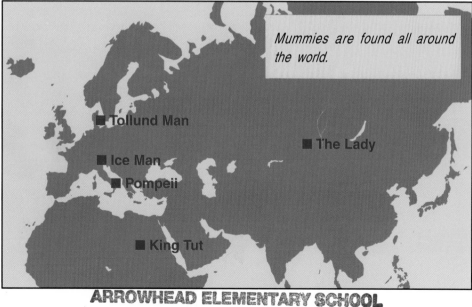

Mummies are found all around the world.

Tollund Man

The Lady

Ice Man

Pompeii

King Tut

The panel of this trunk shows the young pharaoh Tutankhamen and his wife. The pharaoh is hunting birds.

3

KING TUT

The little boy was only nine years old. His head was shaved except for a long thin braid that hung down his neck. Like the other boys of Egypt, he wore jeweled earrings that dangled down to his shoulders. His eyes were outlined in dark makeup. Because today was special, he wore a linen cloth wrapped tightly around his waist.[1] Today little Tutankhaton would become a god.[2]

Three thousand years ago, Egypt was the most powerful civilization on earth. For centuries the Egyptians had built pyramids and beautiful temples and monuments along the Nile River in the middle of the desert. The country was ruled by a series of kings called pharaohs. Tutankhaton was a member of the royal family. After several relatives died, he was next in line to the throne.

At his coronation, Tut was led by priests into a huge temple.

They sprinkled water from the Nile on him. They wrapped a ceremonial snake around his body. Then they set a huge crown on his head. Because a pharaoh needed a queen, he was married to Ankhesenpaaton, a girl who was probably his niece. She was only about twelve years old.[3]

Then the little pharaoh and his queen walked out of the temple and were presented to the people of Egypt. When Tut walked into the sun, everyone in the crowd bowed low. The Egyptians believed in dozens of gods. Now that he was the pharaoh, the nine-year-old boy was a god, too.

Life was good for royal Egyptian children. The boys wrestled and swam and shot arrows from bows. They rolled dice and moved playing pieces around a board game called senet. Little children played with wooden spark-makers. Since he was in the

This senet game was found in Tutankhamen's tomb. Many Egyptian children enjoyed playing this game.

royal family, Tut had learned to read and write in the complicated picture language called hieroglyphics. He also could add, subtract, and multiply.[4]

After he became pharaoh, Tutankhaton probably had no more time for senet or for playing with other boys. His days were spent with priests and tutors. When he was still young, the country was ruled by his advisors, but even they had to bow down to the little pharaoh. As Tut got older, he was given more and more responsibility. Soon he would be running the country on his own. As they became teenagers, Tut and Ankhesenpaaton fell in love and had at least two children. The priests convinced the royal couple to change their names to Tutankhamen and Ankhesenamen to honor the chief Egyptian god, Amon.[5]

By the time he was seventeen or eighteen, Tut should have been able to look forward to growing old with his queen and their children. He wanted to keep his nation strong and happy, but suddenly he died, and Ankhesenamen married an old priest named Ay, who became the new pharaoh. Within a few generations the boy king was almost totally forgotten.

The Pharaoh Is Found

In 1916 a British archaeologist named Howard Carter came to Egypt looking for what was left of Tutankhamen 3,200 years after the pharaoh's death. Carter knew that the ancient Egyptians had buried their pharaohs in tombs cut out of rocky hills in the desert. They surrounded the bodies with gold and jewels. The tombs were so filled with treasures that they were targets of thieves for thousands of years. After careful study, Carter decided that the tombs of all the pharaohs except Tutankhamen had been looted thousands of years before. He was convinced that Tut was still buried in an undiscovered tomb in the Valley of the Kings.

For six years, the archaeologist and his crew carefully shifted through two hundred thousand tons of sand and stone, and came up empty-handed. Then on November 4, 1922, they found a series of steps carved into the rock. Carter's workers emptied the stairway of sand and rocks and realized they had at last found the final resting place of Tutankhamen.

The tomb wasn't just a hole for the body—it was four rooms cut into the side of the hill. The rooms were filled with golden statues and chests and beautiful vases. There was also a chariot the king had used and the feathers of a bird he had killed hunting. On the sides of chests and the back of a golden throne were pictures of Tut and Ankhesenamen. There was also a little chair he had used when he was a boy as well as a toy lighter and a game of senet.

One of the rooms was filled with a wooden box covered with gold. Inside, Carter found a stone box we call a sarcophagus. When the top was removed, he found a wooden coffin, covered with gold, in the shape of a body. Inside of it was another wooden coffin, just a little smaller, but also covered with gold. Inside that one was the third and final coffin, but it wasn't made of wood. It was built out of solid gold.

Opening the Golden Coffin

Inside the third coffin, Carter finally found what he was looking for. There was the pharaoh's body wrapped in yards and yards of linen. Over the top of it was a beautiful gold death mask decorated with hundreds of jewels. Each of his fingers was wrapped in a gold tube. Daggers,

Tut is one of the few royal mummies that was left virtually intact. His golden death mask stunned the world when it was discovered in 1922.

rings, bracelets, collars, and jewels were wrapped in the linen that circled his body.

When Carter finished taking off the linen, he could finally see what was left of Tutankhamen's body. The king had been only about five feet, four inches tall. His ears were pierced, and his head and chin had been carefully shaved. His liver, lungs, stomach, and intestines had been removed and were found in tiny coffins in another room of the tomb. His shriveled heart was the only organ left in his body.

Tut's skin was brittle and discolored, but it was still there, and it covered his body. The Egyptians had kept the body from decomposing by storing it for two months in salt. That removed all the moisture before it was wrapped up in linen. The body would have been in much better shape if the priests had not drenched it with dark oil we call unguents. Over the centuries they had combined with the linen to make a dark, sticky mess.

The pharaoh's body was preserved because his people believed he was setting off on a long journey. He would be reborn in the land of the dead. His tomb was filled with his possessions. The rooms were stuffed full of furniture, toys, weapons, and clothes. There was even a box of loincloths. So he wouldn't be hungry, many baskets of food lined the wall. Since he would need servants in his new life, hundreds of tiny statues called ushabtis were scattered throughout the tomb. In the land of the dead, they would come to life and go to work.

The Death of a God

Tut was well prepared for the land of the dead, but how exactly did he die? In the thousands of hiero-glyphics found written and carved in the tomb, there is no mention of what happened to him. Carter found a small scar on the pharaoh's cheek. Maybe he had been wounded in battle or hurt in an accident. It took further testing and modern X rays to reveal something else. Tut's skull was damaged. He was probably killed by something that banged into his head. Experts today believe he was murdered.[6] Who would want to kill a god? Nobody knows for sure.

Today Tutankhamen lies once again in the Valley of the Kings. His body is back in the tomb resting inside one of his caskets. Meanwhile his treasures have appeared in museums all over the world. The murdered boy king has become the most famous ancient Egyptian of them all.

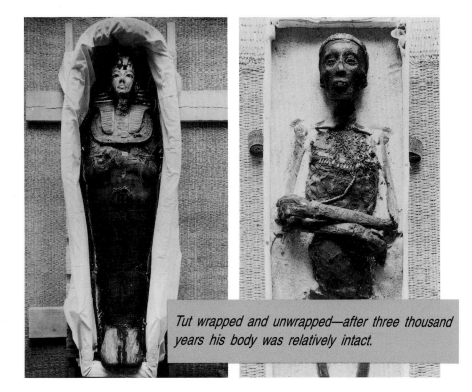

Tut wrapped and unwrapped—after three thousand years his body was relatively intact.

This is a portion of a mural found in a Pompeian villa—as fresh today as when it was painted nearly two thousand years ago.

4

VICTIMS OF VESUVIUS

More than nineteen hundred years ago, Pompeii was a small Roman city on the Mediterranean Sea. It was a beautiful place to live for its 20,000 people. The weather was almost always warm and sunny. Cool breezes from the Mediterranean kept it from getting too hot. A tall mountain called Vesuvius stood about a mile away.[1]

Perfumes, cloth, and fish sauce were made there. Farmers brought their produce to markets in the city. Ships from all over the Mediterranean landed goods at its docks. Most of the homes had two stories. Almost all of them were built around open courtyards. There was an ampitheater, temples, and gymnasiums. Many shops lined the busy stone streets.

The people of Pompeii had a good life, and they expected it

to continue. Nobody suspected that they were in danger from the pretty green mountain that overlooked their city. Nobody realized that Vesuvius was actually an active volcano. It had never erupted since the town had been built.

The End of Pompeii

Then, on a summer morning in A.D. 79, the earth shook and there was a horrible noise as the top blew off Vesuvius. Smoke and ash poured out of the broken mountain, darkening the sky. Fire was also exploding out of the giant hole. Stones so hot that they were on fire shot into the air.

Terrified people tried to save themselves. One family hid in their cellar. There they were safe from the ash and falling rocks. But poisonous gases had begun to leak out of Vesuvius and the cracks in the ground. The people in the cellar started to faint. One of them finally realized they needed fresh air. He grabbed his key and headed for the door, but he had moved too late. He collapsed before he could open it. All eighteen people in the cellar died.

The eruption interrupted a group of priests eating a breakfast of eggs and fish. As they ran out of town, many of them were crushed by falling columns. The rest ran into a home. All but one were soon smothered by ash. As the sizzling ash seeped through one wall, the sole survivor grabbed a hatchet and broke through the opposite wall. The ash followed, and he had to smash through another wall. He managed to stay ahead of the ash until he finally ran into a wall he couldn't break. Then he too died.

A guard dog yanked at his chain, but he couldn't pull free. The poor animal choked to death as he was buried in ash.

A young girl thought the ash shower would soon end. If she

The thirty feet of ash covering Pompeii preserved the city as it was in A.D. 79 As they did nearly two thousand years ago, buildings line this road leading to Vesuvius.

could just keep it out of her nose and mouth for a few minutes, it would stop, and she would be safe. So she fell to the ground and pulled her dress up over her head, but the ash kept falling, and she was smothered.[2]

For two days the ground shook, and Vesuvius rained death. "At last the darkness thinned. . . ." wrote a survivor. "We were terrified to see everything changed, buried deep in ashes like snowdrifts."[3] In places the ash was thirty feet deep. Pompeii was gone.

Victims Are Forgotten

After a few years, grass and trees began growing over the city. People forgot it had ever even existed. Then, almost seventeen centuries later, in 1748, a farmer digging in a vineyard found a buried wall. Soon workers began uncovering the ancient doomed city. The work has continued now for almost two hundred fifty years. Today, the ashes have been cleared away. Visitors can walk the ancient streets and look at the many walls and columns that weren't wrecked by the eruption.

Plaster casts preserve the harrowing last moments of the unlucky citizens of Pompeii who did not escape.

An Italian archaeologist, Giuseppe Fiorelli, was the man who made it possible for us to feel the agony of Vesuvius's victims. In 1864, he discovered that the ash had hardened around their bodies. When the bodies decayed, they left perfect molds surrounding their bones. Fiorelli poured plaster into the molds. When it hardened, he chipped away the ash. That left a white plaster mummy filled with bones, showing exactly how the victims had appeared when they died.

Hundreds of the mummies have been prepared by Fiorelli and more recent archaeologists. These plaster mummies aren't of as much interest to scientists as the Iceman or King Tut. The skin and organs have totally decomposed, and the bones are stuck inside the plaster. The teeth are visible on those who died gasping or screaming for breath, but no other body parts can be inspected.

What we are left with is a horrifying moment frozen forever by ash and then plaster. From these mummies, we are not able to tell much about the diet or the health or the lives of the people of Pompeii, but they do give us a very accurate picture of how these unfortunate people died.

Even though they are made of plaster, the mummies of Pompeii seem more real to most of us because they look like real people. The terrified, twisted dog still seems to be struggling for his life nearly two thousand years after he died. We wish that the ash had not been as thick so that the little girl with the dress pulled over her head could have run to safety. Their mummies, and those of the people who died with them, help us to understand what it must have been like to have been in Pompeii that terrible day.

In some parts of Europe, peat is used as fuel. Digging a trench like this one, two Danish brothers found the body of a man they thought had been recently murdered.

♦ 5 ♦

TOLLUND MAN

It was early spring and the weather was still cool, but the man wore only a cap, a belt, and a rope around his neck. He tried not to react when the ends of the rope were twisted. He knew what was coming.[1] The noose got tighter and tighter, and soon he was dead. Finally the rope was loosened, and his limp body was lowered into a soggy black bog.

On May 8, 1950, two brothers, Emil and Viggo Hojgaard, were near the same spot in Tollund Fen, Denmark, digging up peat, a dark soil formed by layers and layers of dead plants packed down in soggy ground. The brothers cut the peat into chunks so that it could be dried and then burned as fuel.

Everything was fine until they got down about seven feet. Then their spades struck something hard. Looking down, they saw the head of a dead man, wearing a cap. When police arrived at the bog, they noticed that the man's face seemed to be an unnatural reddish-brown. Tollund Man, as he would soon be known, appeared to be sleeping. The police suspected that he had recently fallen or been shoved into the bog.

A Murder Long Ago

Professor Peter Glob arrived and quickly discovered the rope wrapped around Tollund Man's neck. The ends hung down his back. It was obvious he had been killed. But who had done it? And who exactly was Tollund Man? Nobody around Tollund Fen recognized his face.

Glob took the body and the peat that surrounded it to Copenhagen's National Museum. The first thing he noticed was that the man was only wearing a belt, a cap, and the rope. Not all of his body was as well preserved as the head, and some of his bones were showing, but his internal organs were in great shape.

Over the next several weeks, Glob began to unravel the mystery of Tollund Man. It was obvious he wasn't accustomed to tough physical work, because his hands and feet were soft, and his fingernails weren't broken. By examining the stomach and intestines, Glob determined that Tollund Man's last meal had been a porridge made out of grains and seeds.

The condition of the teeth led the professor to believe that he was at least twenty years old. There was stubble on his chin. His hair was short—about two inches long. It was red—just like his skin.

Glob was able to report conclusively that a murder had been committed, but he told the police not to bother looking for the

The tannic acid in the peat bog preserved Tollund Man's skin, hair, and hat. The head, feet, and internal organs were especially well preserved.

murderers. The "crime" had taken place almost two thousand years before. The victim himself had probably wanted to die.[2]

The Goddess Demands a Sacrifice

Tollund Man, the professor explained, had lived about the time Jesus Christ was alive in Palestine. The people around the Tollund bog worshiped many gods and goddesses. One of the most powerful was Nerthus, the goddess of fertility, whose symbol was a twisted rope. If she was happy, the people would have a successful harvest. If she was angry, the crops wouldn't grow and the people might starve. Their religious customs had been described by the Roman historian Tacitus 1,900 years ago.

The ancient farmers around Tollund figured they knew how to keep Nerthus happy. One of the men was picked each year to be her husband. That was why his hands were soft. He had been worshiped as a god, and he did not have to work, but at the end of a religious festival, his time was up. He was sacrificed to his "wife," Nerthus, strangled by the twisted rope that was her symbol.[3] Glob knew that bodies of other sacrificial victims had been found in Denmark and other Scandinavian countries. Many of them had also been strangled.

There were no scratches or other evidence of a struggle on Tollund Man's body. He had wanted to die. It was his duty. Besides, his was a good bargain. After being strangled, he believed that he would be with the goddess forever, and his death would guarantee a fine harvest for his people. His sacrifice would help keep them alive another year.[4]

The Bog Preserves the Body

After his death Tollund Man's body was lowered into the sacred bog. His people had no way of knowing that burying him there would preserve his body for thousands of years. A bog is a soggy low area from which water cannot drain. Layers and layers of dead plants build up on the bottom under the water. Over the years the plants are packed down and decay. They turn into peat, which looks like black dirt.

The peaceful look on the Tollund Man's face has led some to believe that the man was a willing sacrifice.

Moss grows over the soggy bog, trapping the water under the surface. That causes the water to lose its oxygen. The moss gives off acid that kills bacteria. Without oxygen and bacteria in the water, nothing in the bog can decay. It just turns red. The bog becomes a mummy-maker, and bodies in it can last forever.

Not All the Victims Wanted to Die

Many other bodies have been discovered in the bogs of Denmark and other European countries. Some of them apparently weren't as ready as Tollund Man to die. At least one struggled, and the rope around his neck wasn't enough to kill him. His throat was slit, and his skull was bashed in.

Today the head of Tollund Man is on display in Silkeborg, Denmark. Visitors can come face to face with a man who died two thousand years ago. They can look at his calm, peaceful expression and wonder if they would have had the courage to face death as he did.

After tons of rocks forming the kurgan were removed, the Lady's ice-covered tomb was revealed. In the right foreground are the remains of the horses buried with her.

6

THE LADY

It was spring, time for the Pazyryks to leave the Pastures of Heaven. But first the burial had to be completed. The ground had thawed so they could dig the pit and line it with logs. Chunks of mutton and horsemeat were left to provide nourishment on the way to the new life. The mummy itself was laid on its side in a coffin made from a hollowed log.

The body had been prepared for its journey. The skull had been broken open and the brain removed. All the internal organs and muscles had been scraped away. The Pazyryks then stuffed the body with herbs, grasses, and wool and sewed it back together.

At the edge of the pit stood six horses dressed in beautiful harnesses. The sheep, the rest of the horses, and the Pazyryks would soon be leaving for the summer pastures, but the decorated horses would not. As they waited, a strong man picked up a heavy pointed ax and walked toward them. Suddenly he smashed it into the skull of one of the horses. One at a time the others were killed and lowered into the pit. They, too, would be needed on the way to the new life.

A wooden lid was placed over the log walls, forming a small room around the coffin. Then the pit was refilled with dirt. On top was a kurgan, a mound of rocks. The Pazyryks took their sheep and the rest of the horses and left the Pastures of Heaven.

"The End of Everything"

In the summer of 1993, 2,400 years later, Natalya Polosmak, a Russian archaeologist, brought her students to the steppes of Siberia. This is an area of cold, treeless plains surrounded on three sides by China, Mongolia, and Kazakhstan. The Siberians call it Ukok, "the end of everything."[1] No roads lead to the steppes, and there are no nearby towns. The only way to get to Ukok is a five-hour helicopter ride.

Polosmak knew Ukok had once been used as winter pastures by the Pazyryks, an ancient nomadic tribe. The winter winds were so strong that they blew away all the snow, leaving bare frozen grass for their sheep. The Pazyryks thought of Ukok as the closest spot on the world to heaven.[2] They called the area, "the Pastures of Heaven."

Polosmak led her crew to a kurgan. Under the mound of rocks, she expected to find at least traces of a Pazyryk burial chamber. Since the kurgans were so visible, she knew that many of them had been looted by tribes that came later. This time she was lucky. When the rocks and dirt were cleared away, there was the unbroken lid of a chamber. No one had been inside for twenty-four centuries!

The archaeologist knew the most she could expect to find was a skeleton and a few artifacts. When the lid was removed, all she could see was ice. Sometime after the burial, the entire chamber had filled with water that was still frozen. If the chamber had been soaked in water for any length of time, almost everything inside would probably be ruined.

Polosmak wondered when the water had entered the chamber. If it had leaked in soon after the burial and frozen very quickly, everything inside would be very well preserved. She realized there wasn't much chance of the crew being that lucky.

The Ice Melts

With the lid off, the sun warmed the chamber for the first time in centuries. Soon the ice began turning to mush. To speed the melting, Polosmak poured hot water onto the ice. Soon she could see a long wooden coffin, then two small tables holding mutton and horsemeat. Since the food hadn't completely rotted away, Polosmak knew it must have frozen very quickly after the burial. As the hot water hit the meat, it formed a kind of hot soup. Polosmak could smell the 2,400-year-old meal.

As the deeper ice turned to mush, she could see the rotting bodies of the six decorated horses. Pieces of their brown coats still hung to their bones. Each of them had a hole in its skull made by the blow of the ax. Soon their thawed bodies began to stink in the sun.

Polosmak turned her attention to the coffin. When long bronze nails were pulled out, the lid could be removed. Inside was a solid block of dark ice. She wondered what would be left of the dead Pazyryk. She knew the body would have been damaged when the skull was split and the organs removed, but she hoped that what was left hadn't had a chance to decompose before freezing.

As she poured hot water from a cup onto the ice inside the coffin, the archaeologist could begin to see shapes emerge. The first thing she recognized was a jawbone. Then, as more ice melted, a chunk of flesh on a cheek was revealed.

Soon the whole mummy was free of the ice, and Polosmak could see it was covered by a fur blanket. When she pulled back the blanket she could see the body wore a flowing woolen skirt and a silk tunic. It also had a long wooden headdress decorated by eight carved cats covered with gold. The mummy had been a noble woman. Polosmak called her "The Lady."

Much of the body was still covered by soft skin. Her long fingers looked like they belonged on the body of a strong young woman, not on someone who had been dead for 2,400 years. When Polosmak pulled the blanket back from one of the hands, she found a dark blue tattoo of a deer on the Lady's wrist. Under the tunic was another tattoo on her shoulder. It was a strange design of a mythical creature with long, swirling horns.

Polosmak knew she had been very lucky. The Lady's burial chamber had obviously been flooded by rain or melting snow very soon after it had been sealed. Almost immediately the water had frozen, preserving what was left of the horses, the meal, and the Lady herself.

Who Was She? The archaeologist decided she must have been very important to her people. Why else would she have been given such a special burial? The

Pazyryks could not have left six horses in the tombs of every dead member of the tribe. The Lady must have done something very special to deserve such treatment.

There are still many questions about the tomb in the Pastures of Heaven. What was the meaning of the tattoos? Was the headdress some kind of crown? How had the Lady died? Polosmak admitted, "What we know is not everything."[3]

The mummy of the Lady was flown from Ukok by helicopter to Moscow, Russia, where it is still being investigated by scientists. Meanwhile Natalya Polosmak is looking for more mummies and other traces of the ancient Pazyryks. The search for answers goes on.

The Lady's left arm is covered with tattoos of fabulous animals and symbols.

Chapter 1

1. Konrad Spindler, *The Man in the Ice,* (New York: Harmony Books, 1994).The events described here are the theoretical last moments of the Iceman as described by Spindler, leader of the scientific team that has examined the body.

2. Sandy Fritz, "Who Was the Iceman?," *Popular Science,* vol. 242, no. 2 (February 1993), p. 46.

3. David Roberts, "The Ice Man: Lone Visitor From the Copper Age," *National Geographic,* vol. 184, no. 6 (June 1993), p. 47.

4. Fritz, p. 50.

Chapter 2

1. Robin McKie, "Probers Study Mummies for Clues of Past," *Detroit Free Press,* September 18, 1994, p. 12A.

Chapter 3

1. Katharine Stoddert Gilbert, with Joan K. Holt and Sara Hudson (editors), *Treasures of Tutankhamun,* (New York: Metropolitan Museum of Art, 1976), p. 125.

2. Christiane Desroches-Noblecourt, *Tutankamen* (Boston: New York Graphic Society, 1976), p. 170.

3. Ibid, pp. 163, 170.

4. Cyril Aldred, *Tutankhamen's Egypt* (New York: Charles Scribners' Sons, 1972), p.46.

5. I.E.S. Edwards, *The Treasures of Tutankhamun* (Middlesex, England: Penguin Books, Ltd., 1972), p. 18

6. Nicholas Reeves, *The Complete Tutankhamun* (New York: Thames and Hudson, Inc., 1990), p. 118.

Chapter 4

1. Alfonso de Franciscis, *Pompeii—The Excavations* (Naples, Italy: Interdipress, 19, undated), p. 5.

2. Kathryn Long Humphrey, *Pompeii—Nightmare at Midday* (New York Franklin Watts, 1990), p. 31.

3. Ron and Nancy Goor, *Pompeii: Exploring a Roman Ghost Town* (New York: Thomas Y. Crowell, 1986), p. ix.

Notes by Chapter

Chapter 5

1. P. V. Glob, "Lifelike Man Preserved 2,000 Years in Peat," *National Geographic,* vol. 105, no. 3 (March 1954), p. 419.

2. Ibid.

3. Maurice Shadbolt, "Who Killed the Bog Men of Denmark? And Why?," *Reader's Digest,* vol. 110, no. 662 (June 1977), p. 204.

4. Glob, p. 428

Chapter 6

1. Natalya Polosmak, "A Mummy Unearthed From the Pastures of Heaven," *National Geographic,* vol. 186, no. 4 (October 1994), p. 87.

2. Ibid.

3. "Ice Tombs of Siberia," *National Geographic Explorer,* TBS, originally broadcast October 9, 1994.

c. **500,000** B.C.—Modern Humans (*Homo sapiens*) appear.

c. **8000** B.C.—The first cities are founded.

c. **5000** B.C.—The oldest known Egyptian mummy.

c. **3200** B.C.—Copper Age begins in Europe.

c. **3100** B.C.—Old Kingdom of Egypt begins.

c. **3000** B.C.—The Iceman dies.

c. **2500** B.C.—The great pyramids of Egypt are built.

c. **2300** B.C.—Bronze Age begins in Europe.

c. **1342** B.C.—Tutankhhaton is born.

c. **1332** B.C.—Tutankhhaton becomes Pharoah Tutankhamen.

c. **1323** B.C.—Tutankhamen dies.

c. **800** B.C.—First settlement of Pompeii.

753 B.C.—The legendary date of the founding of Rome.

c.**700–100** B.C.—Pazyryks roamed the plains of Central Asia.

c. **400** B.C.—"The Lady" is buried in Siberia.

c. **300** B.C.—Pompeii is conquered by Rome.

A List of Important Dates

B.C.

A.D.

c. **50**—Death of Tollund Man.

79—Mount Vesuvius erupts and buries the Roman cities of Pompeii, Herculaneum, and Stabiae.

1748—Pompeii is rediscovered.

1864—The first casts of Pompeii's victims are made.

1922—Harold Carter discovers Tutankhamen's tomb.

1950—Two brothers discover the body of the Tollund Man in a peat bog in Tollund Fen, Denmark.

1991—The Iceman is discovered.

1993—A Russian team of archaeologists discovers "The Lady" near Ukok, Siberia.

Amon—The chief god of the ancient Egyptians.

archaeologist—A scientist who studies past human cultures and civilizations in order to understand how they lived.

bacteria—A group of mostly single-celled organisms, identified by their lack of a cell nucleus.

bog—Wet, spongy ground that usually forms when decaying plant growth fills in a swamp.

coronation—The official ceremony crowning a ruler.

decompose—To decay. When an organism dies, other organisms feed on the remains until there is virtually nothing left.

embalm—To preserve a human body.

forensics—Investigation though medical examinations.

formaldehyde—A chemical used to preserve the bodies of dead animals.

glacier—In cold climates, accumulated snowfall builds up creating a year-round mass of ice, especially on mountaintops. Since ice expands as it freezes, glaciers can grow and shrink.

heiroglyphics—A form of writing that uses pictures to symbolize words and sounds.

kurgan—A burial mound.

longbow—A large bow, often up to six feet in length.

mutton—The meat of an older sheep.

Nerthus—An ancient fertility goddess of the Celtic people of Europe.

nomadic—People, or animals, that regularly travel from place to place in search of food and shelter.

Pazyryks—An ancient nomadic people of Central Asia. Little is known about them, except that they were excellent horsemen. The Pazyryks are thought to be related to another more well-known group, the Scythians.

peat—The remains of plants that have decayed and become compacted beneath a swamp. After many years, the material becomes almost like coal, and can be burned as fuel.

pharaoh—The name give to the male rulers of ancient Egypt.

porridge—Grains or beans boiled in milk or water to form a food that is similar to oatmeal.

sarcophagus—A large stone coffin.

senet—A game of the ancient Egyptians.

tunic—A loose-fitting slip-on garment, worn by ancient peoples, especially the Romans and Greeks.

unguents—Ointments used to anoint the body and moisturize the skin.

ushabtis—Tiny statues placed in Egyptian tombs. In the afterlife, they were supposed to come to life to work for the mummy in the Land of the Dead.

Barloy, Jean-Jacques. *Prehistory*. Hauppauge, N.Y.: Barron's Educational Series, Inc., 1987.

Brothwell, Don R. *The Bog Man & the Archaeology of People*. Cambridge, Mass.: Harvard University Press, 1990.

Chrisp, Peter. *The Romans*. New York: Chelsea House Publishers, 1994.

Dunrea, Oliver. *Skara Brae: The Story of a Prehistoric Village*. New York: Holiday House, 1986.

Further Reading

Harris, Geraldine. *Gods & Pharaohs from Egyptian Mythology*. New York: Peter Bedrick Books, 1992.

Hart, George. *Ancient Egypt*. New York: Harcourt Brace & Company, 1989.

Hicks, Peter. *The Romans*. New York: Thomson Learning, 1994.

Morley, Jacqueline and John James. *A Roman Villa: Inside Story*. New York: Peter Bedrick Books, 1992.

Scheller, William. *Amazing Archaeologists & Their Finds*. Minneapolis: The Oliver Press, 1994.

Index

L

DATE DUE			

Bound to Stay Bound Books, Inc.